I Spy
with My Little
Eye
Hockey

Photographs by **David Milne** and text by **Matt Napier**

Fun for all ages!

Sleeping Bear Press

To my wife Linda and daughters Lindsay, Heather and Katie

D. M.

To Krista - my wife, my friend and my daily inspiration

M. N.

David Milne would like to thank:
MARK AND JAN NAPIER
ADAM BISSONNETTE
CHRIS SOUCY, ETOBICOKE DOLPHINS
RON SIMPSON
STEVE NASH, EYECANDYAIR
TORONTO MAPLE LEAFS
CANADIAN ICE ACADEMY
VINCENT AND ADRIENNE CARNOVALE
DEREK VANDERVINNE
THE CARUANA FAMILY-especially MACK
GOALIE HEAVEN, TORONTO
PLAY IT AGAIN SPORTS, ETOBICOKE
BERNARD ATHLETIC KNIT, TORONTO

Text Copyright © 2008 Matt Napier
Photographs Copyright © 2008 David Milne

Sleeping Bear Press™

315 E. Eisenhower Pkwy., Suite 200
Ann Arbor, MI 48108
www.sleepingbearpress.com

Sleeping Bear Press is an imprint of Gale, a part of Cengage Learning.

10 9 8 7 6 5

Library of Congress Cataloging-in-Publication Data Napier, Matt.
I spy with my little eye. Hockey / written by Matt Napier ; photographs by David Milne.
p.cm.
Summary: "Each page includes two photos related to hockey. Using poetic clues, readers try to spy the changes made from the original photo on the left to the altered photo on the right. Subjects include skate sharpening, referees, jerseys, and trophies"—Provided by publisher.
ISBN 978-1-58536-365-0
1. Hockey—Juvenile literature. 2. Picture puzzles—Juvenile literature. I. Milne, David, photographer .
II. Title. III. Title: Hockey.
GV847.25.N353 2008
796.962—dc22   2008022954

Printed by China Translation & Printing Services Limited, Guangdong Province, China. 5th printing. 09/2011

I spy with my little eye, two pictures that look just the same.
An identical view isn't always what's true.
Find the changes to play this game.

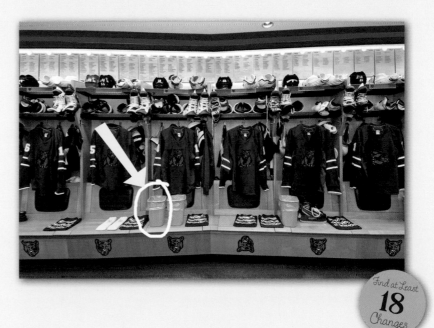

Find at Least
18
Changes

Now let's get started...

I spy with my little eye, a new hockey game starting up.
Players skate on, the puck moves along, and everyone vies for the Cup.

Find at Least

38

Changes

Photo Fact: The first hockey cards appeared between 1910 and 1913, prior to World War I. After the war, some food and candy companies began including cards with purchases of their product on a limited basis. Many hockey cards produced today include interesting information about the player, including height, weight, and season statistics.

I spy with my little eye, a practice and skates being tied.
Players take shots, a wall gains some spots, and a goalie moves side to side.

Find at Least **21** Changes

Photo Fact: Believe it or not, hockey rinks are not all created equal in size! Most North American rinks, including those used by NHL teams, have ice surfaces that are slightly smaller than rinks found in the rest of the world. Practice is a time to work on the skills that players need to use in a game. Coaches will have players do all kinds of drills to help improve their skating, shooting, and stick handling. You know what they say: practice makes perfect!

I spy with my little eye, a dressing room where changes abound.
Logos rotate, a triplicate skate, and the captain can no longer be found.

Find at Least **18** Changes

Photo Fact: The captain is the team's leader on and off the ice. You can identify the captain by the "C" on his or her jersey. Teams also have a few alternate captains, generally 2 or 3, who wear an "A" on their jerseys. Some famous NHL captains include Steve Yzerman, who holds the record as the NHL's longest serving captain (he wore the "C" for 20 seasons with the Detroit Red Wings), and Sidney Crosby, who at the age of 19 was named the captain of the Pittsburgh Penguins – the youngest permanent captain in the history of the NHL. Some famous women's hockey captains include Cassie Campbell and Haley Wickenheiser of the Canadian National team and Cammie Granato of the U.S. National team.

I spy with my little eye, women and girls on the ice.
The home team moves away, some colours stray, look up to the scoreboard twice.

Find at Least
22
Changes

Photo Fact: Women have been playing organized ice hockey in North America for almost as long as men. One of the earliest photos of a women's hockey game dates back to around 1890. In fact, Lord Stanley of Preston (the man who donated the cup awarded to "the championship hockey club of the Dominion of Canada" – you'd recognize it as the Stanley Cup) had a daughter named Isobel who is one of the first women to be photographed with a puck and stick.

I spy with my little eye, equipment scattered all over the ground.
Bottles change places, some moving skate laces, an "L" can no longer be found.

Find at Least
36
Changes

Photo Fact: The equipment has changed a lot since hockey was first played. In fact, considering organized ice hockey has been played for well over 150 years (and by some accounts a lot longer than that!), helmets are a relatively new development. It was not common for forwards and defencemen to wear helmets until the 1970s. Even goalies did not wear masks in the early years of the game.

I spy with my little eye, goalie helmets galore!
See the stars with your eyes, and eagles that fly; count thirteen changes or more.

Find at Least 18 Changes

Photo Fact: Jacque Plante was the first goalie to wear a mask every game, after a puck cut his face in 1959. Even then, it was not until well into the 1960s that most goalies began to wear masks full time. Now, all goalies wear masks and many professionals choose to decorate their masks with artwork representing their team, their personalities, or with other interesting designs. Many of these designs are works of art unto themselves and professional mask painters spend days or even weeks making sure the designs are just right.

I spy with my little eye, a hockey winter wonderland.
Some things move again: a shovel, an "M", and a stick disappears from a hand.

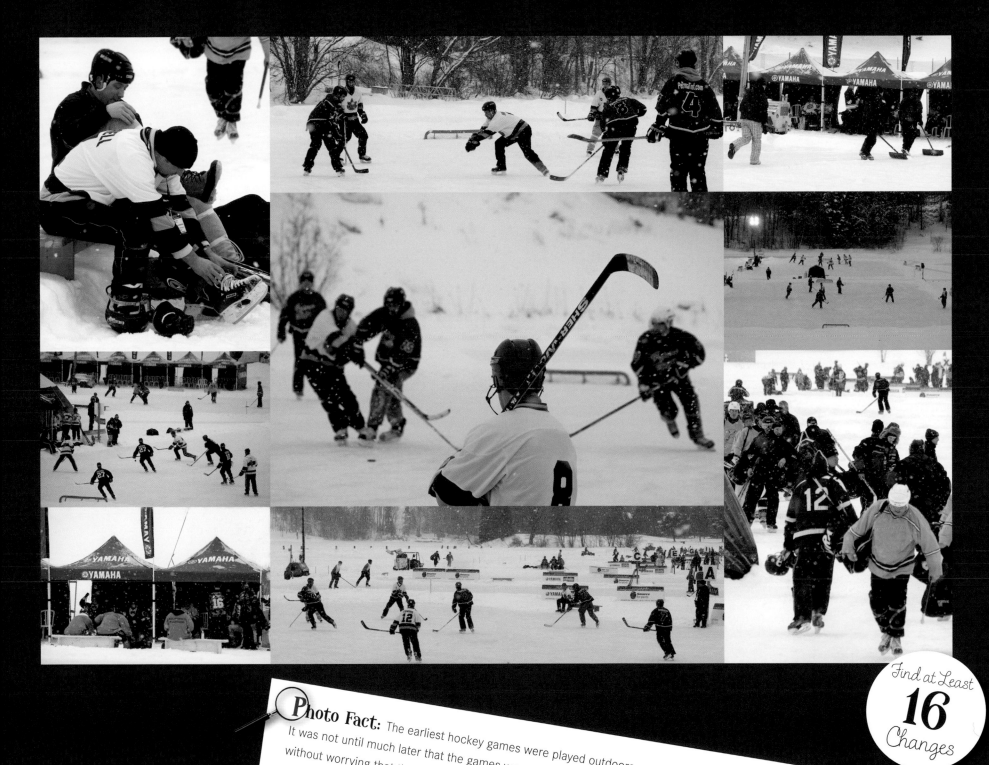

Find at Least **16** Changes

Photo Fact: The earliest hockey games were played outdoors, on frozen ponds, lakes and rivers. It was not until much later that the games were moved inside to enclosed areas where fans could watch without worrying that the game could be cancelled because of a blizzard! Despite the existence of indoor arenas, many people choose to play pond hockey when the weather permits. In the past few years, the NHL has even organized two regular season games played in outdoor arenas. The Heritage Classic was played in 2003 between the Montreal Canadiens and the Edmonton Oilers. The Winter Classic was played in 2008 between the Buffalo Sabres and the Pittsburgh Penguins.

I spy with my little eye, hockey treasures from the past.
A "nine" turns to "six", keep your eye on the sticks, and a Zamboni® that drives away fast.

Find at Least
39
Changes

🔍 **Photo Fact:** Among the many storied NHL franchises, the Montreal Canadiens have won the most Stanley Cups, a total of 23. The player who has won the most Hart trophies as the NHL regular season most valuable player is Wayne Gretzky with 9. In international competition, both Canada and the Soviet Union share the honour of having won the most Olympic gold medals in men's ice hockey. Each country has won 7 gold medals. On the women's side, Canada tops the list with 2 Olympic gold medal wins, narrowly beating the one gold medal won by the U.S.

I spy with my little eye, referees making calls with their hands.
A cross-check, a slash, time ticks by in a flash, look at the stripes and the bands.

Find at Least
15
Changes

I spy with my little eye, hockey jerseys hung in a row.
Look for numbers that change, colours rearranged, see them all from the minors to pro.

Find at Least
14
Changes

I spy with my little eye, sharpening skates before we play.
Hold the skate really tight, keep the blade in your sight, the sparks — a flashy display.

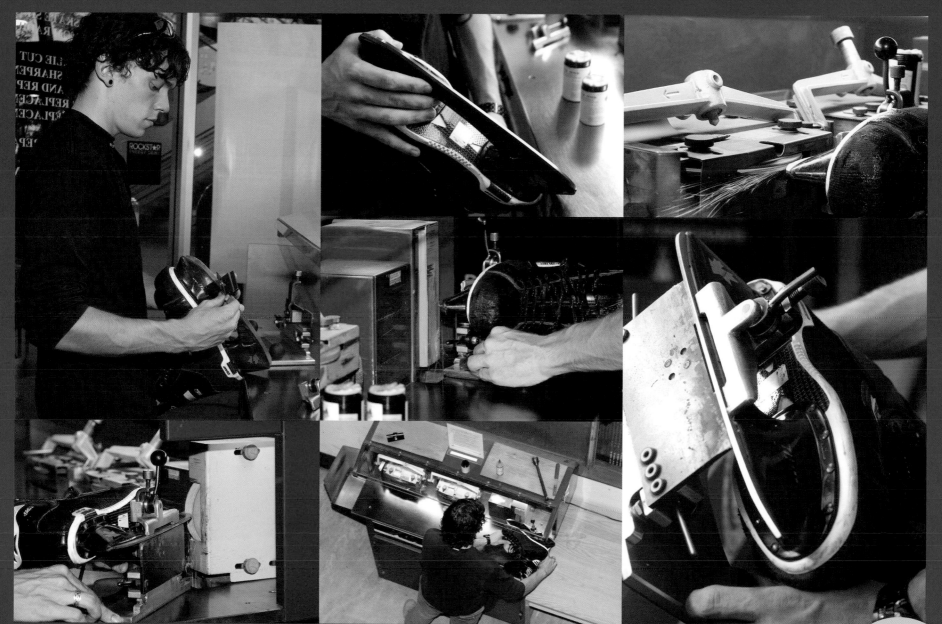

Find at Least **16** Changes

Photo Fact: As technology advances so too does hockey equipment. It is thought that the earliest skate blades were made from animal bones. Eventually, people began making the blades out of polished metal which was fastened to ordinary boots or shoes with leather bindings. It wasn't until much later that skates were manufactured in one piece, with the boot and blade fused together. Skate sharpening is an important part of hockey, although the frequency of the sharpenings differs from player to player. Some players like to have their skates sharpened before every game, while others go many games between sharpenings. If the skate is sharpened incorrectly, the blade could be too dull to dig into the ice, or it could make it more likely that the skate will "catch an edge," causing the player to lose balance or even fall.

I spy with my little eye, trophies and medals and plaques.
Players moved around, shiny bowls upside down, see things turned from front to back.

Find at Least
23
Changes

Photo Fact: Awards for team and individual accomplishments are presented at all levels of hockey. The ultimate trophy is the Stanley Cup, which is now awarded to the winner of the NHL playoffs. The Stanley Cup is kept at the Hockey Hall of Fame in Toronto and the first team to win the Cup was the Montreal Amateur Athletic Association in 1893. The Hockey Hall of Fame is also home to all kinds of incredible hockey memorabilia, history and interactive games. Every true hockey fan should try to visit the Hall of Fame at least once!

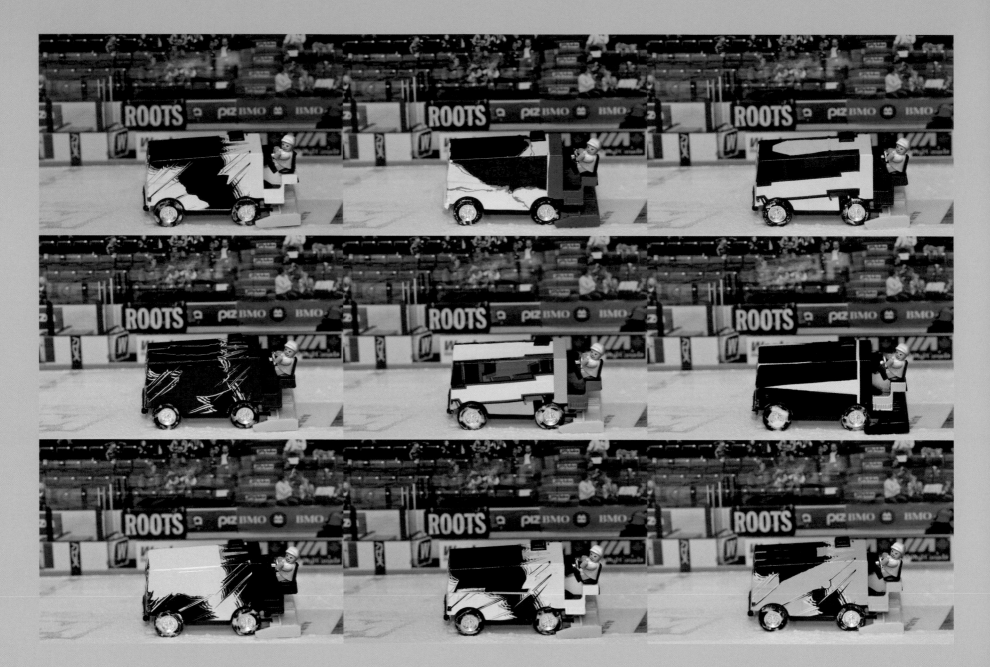

I spy with my little eye ice machines driving to and fro.
They zoom by the fans, as the driver waves his hands; clearing away the snow.

Find at Least **23** Changes

Photo Fact: All of those skate blades carving up the ice leave crevasses and ruts, making the ice uneven and bumpy. The ice needs to be resurfaced between periods and before games to make sure the players have a smooth and clean sheet of ice on which to play. Prior to the invention of the Zamboni® machine the ice was resurfaced by a tractor pulling a scraper to shave the ice. Then several people had to shovel away the shavings, water the ice, remove excess water and then wait for it to freeze. In the 1940s, Frank J. Zamboni invented a machine that did all of this at once. A few other companies now produce ice resurfacing machines, but Zamboni® was the first — and most famous!

I spy with my little eye pucks and sticks placed here and there.
Count pucks on the ground, numbers changed around, look at both and compare.

Find at Least **15** Changes

Photo Fact: Originally, sticks were made primarily out of wood, more recently reinforced with fiber-glass, but now many different materials are used to produce hockey sticks. Some players use aluminum shafts with replaceable wooden blades, while most professionals use "composite" sticks made out of several durable materials often including kevlar and carbon fibre. These new sticks are generally lighter and more durable than their wooden counterparts, although they are also more expensive.

David Milne is a third generation photographer in Toronto, Canada. His grandfather, Charles, started Milne Studios in Toronto in 1925. When David completed his schooling at Brooks Institute of Photography in Santa Barbara, California, he returned home to the family business. Currently David is very active photographing art for numerous Art Galleries and artists, corporate portraits, product and all types of events.

Matt Napier was born in Montreal, Quebec and moved frequently throughout North America and Italy with his family before settling in Toronto, Ontario where he now resides. He recently completed law school at the University of Windsor and is now working for a law firm in Toronto. Matt is also the author of the best-selling **Z is for Zamboni: A Hockey Alphabet** and **Hat Tricks Count: A Hockey Number Book**. When not working or writing, Matt enjoys reading, playing hockey, golfing, and traveling.